Aa

Bb

Cc

Dd

Ee

Ff

Gg

Hh

Ii

Jj

Kk

Ll

Mm

Nn

Asia

NOODLES
Instant

To Susie:
"What do you want to eat?"

Grateful for the ultimate love language shown over and over again -- in every meal we shared together.

- your Little Sister

All inquiries including bulk purchase for promotional, educational, and business events, should be directed to
hello@byyobeqiu.com

byYQ

Published by By Yobe Qiu, LLC 2022

Asian Adventures

DELICIOUS ASIAN FOODS FROM

A - Z!

by Yobe Qiu

Illustrated by Cynthia Li

Aa

is for Asia, the continent
of delicious foods.

Asia

Bb

is for bibimbap, rice mixed
with yummy toppings, served
in hot stone bowls from
Korea.

Cc

is for chili crab, a flavorful
entree from Singapore.

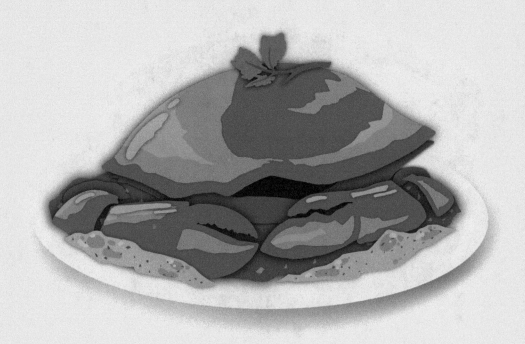

Dd

is for durian, a fruit
so smelly but eaten by
many, native to
Southeast Asia.

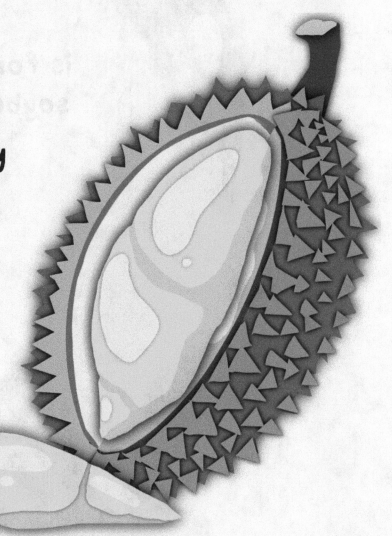

Ee

is for edamame, a healthy soybean snack, still in the bean pod!

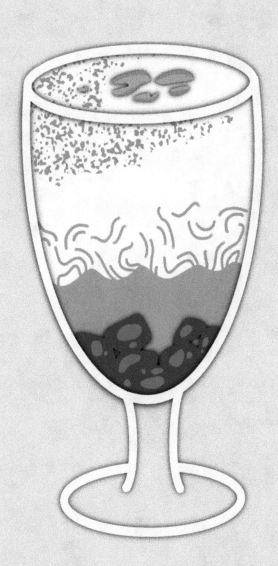

Ff

is for falooda, a colorful
Indian cold dessert made
with noodles.

Gg

is for ginger, a spicy root
used in food and tea.

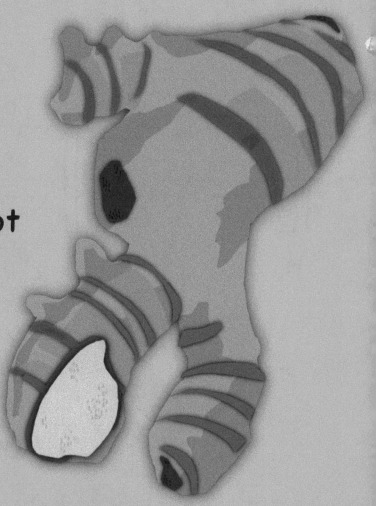

Hh

is for hot pot, joined by friends and families
cooking and eating together.

Ii

is for instant
noodles, a Japanese
creation beloved
worldwide.

Hh

is for hot pot, joined by friends and families
cooking and eating together.

Ii

is for instant noodles, a Japanese creation beloved worldwide.

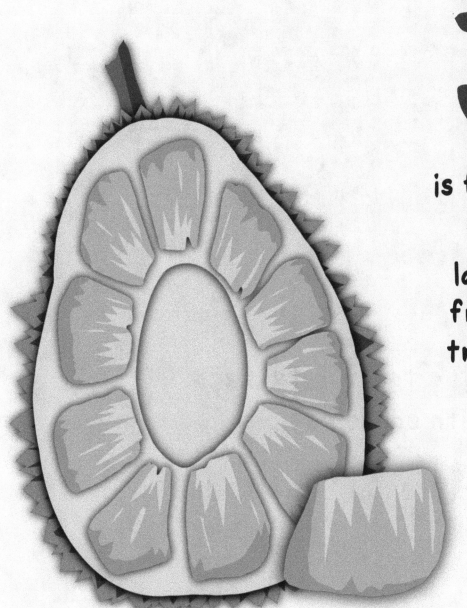

Jj

is for jackfruit, the world's largest edible fruit found in tropical South Asia.

Kk

is for kumquat, a tasty, bite-sized
citrus with edible peel.

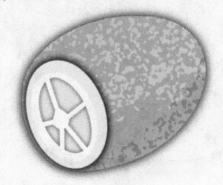

Ll

is for lok lak, also known as Cambodian shaking beef as they dance in the wok!

Mm

is for mooncake, a special treat symbolizing reunion during the Moon Festival.

Nn

is for nattō, a traditional Japanese food made from fermented soy beans.

is for oyster sauce, a staple of Asian home cooking.

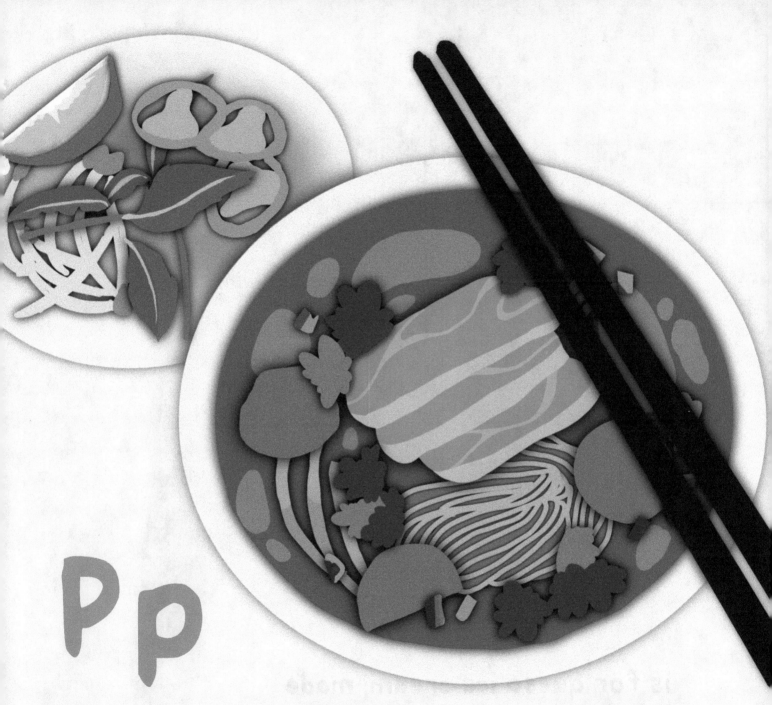

Pp

is for phở, a warm noodle soup, Vietnam's national dish.

Qq

is for queso ice cream, made
in the Philippines with cheese.

Rr

is for roti, a round flatbread native to India.

S s

is for sushi, made by hand
with love from Japan.

Tt

is for Thai iced tea, a bright orange beverage made with condensed milk.

Uu

is for ube, a sweet purple yam from
the Philippines.

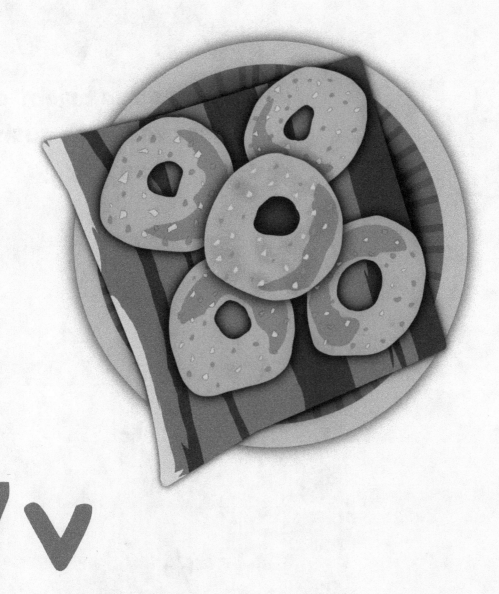

Vv

is for vada, a yummy fried snack from India.

W w

is for wasabi, a bright green
paste served with sushi and
oh so spicy!

X x

is for xiaolongbao, a Chinese pork dumpling with hot soup inside.

Yy

is for yakitori, a Japanese street food of skewered chicken.

Zz

is for zongzi, a traditional Chinese sticky rice dish eaten during Dragon Boat Festival celebrations.

Author

Yobe Qiu is an educator, entrepreneur, mom, and bestselling author with a passion for storytelling. As an educator, Yobe taught children and their families to embrace love and diverse cultures. When she identified a need for more cultural books, she decided to create her own children's stories featuring Asian characters and cultures. Today, Yobe is proud to publish books that help children like her daughter feel seen, heard, and represented. Yobe looks forward to writing many more stories in the years to come.

 hello@byyobeqiu.com   www.byyobeqiu.com

Illustrator

Cynthia Li is an artist working as an illustrator in New York City. she is very passionate about sharing Asian American stories and all things yummy! In her free time, she loves getting inspired by books and movies, as well as eating a good meal. Asian Adventures A-Z Foods is Cynthia Li's debut children's book!

cynthiajiawenli@gmail.com

Yobe Qiu is the Author of

Asian Adventures A-Z
I Am An Amazing Asian Girl
Our Lunar New Year
Our Moon Festival
Our Double Fifth Celebration
The Asian Holidays Children's Activity Book

If you enjoyed this book, or any of Yobe Qiu's books, please leave a review. Your kindness and support are greatly appreciated!

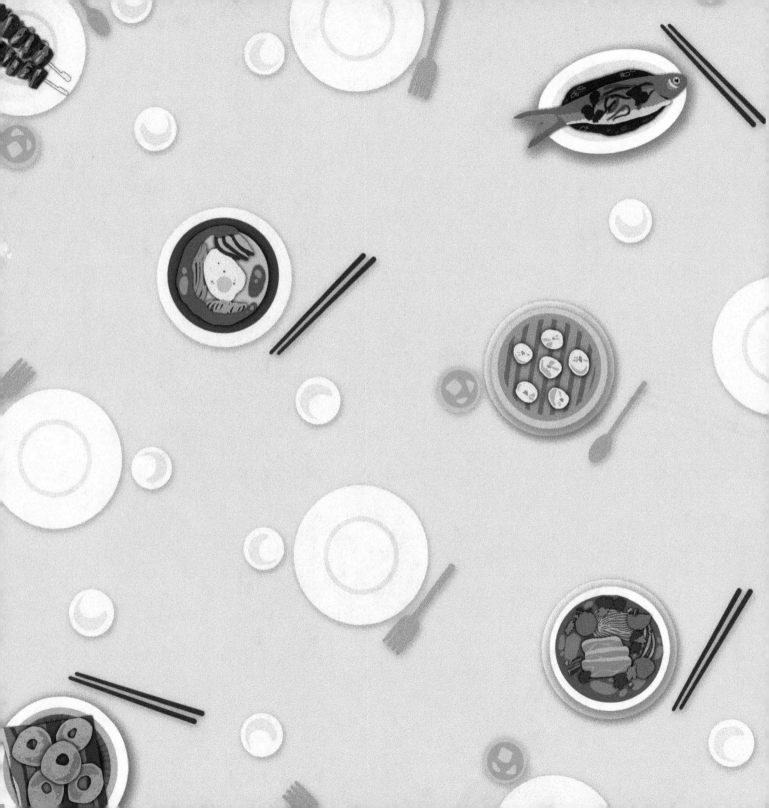

Printed in the USA
CPSIA information can be obtained
at www.ICGtesting.com
LVHW010448160923
758119LV00059B/13